FROM THE HEAVENS FALL THE FAIR BRIGHT STARS

Published by The Onslaught Press
Teach an tSléibhe, Mín a' Lea
on 1 May 2019

Monotypes & design © 2019 **Ian Joyce & Mathew Staunton**
Text © 2019 **Mathew Staunton**

All rights reserved. No part of this publication may be reproduced, stored in a retrieval system, or transmitted, in any form or by any means, electronic, mechanical, photocopying, recording, or otherwise, without the prior permission in writing of the publisher, or as expressly permitted by law, or under terms agreed with the appropriate reprographics rights organization

ISBN: **978-1-912111-93-0**

The text is set in **DIN Next** by Akira Kobayashi

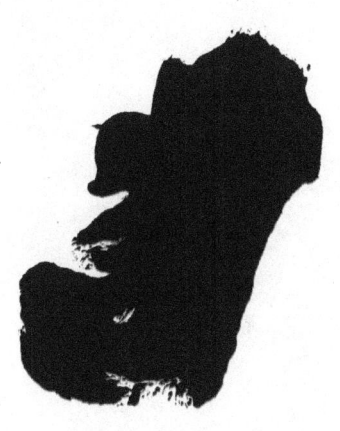

I AM WRITING THESE WORDS IN THE GALLEY OF A LITTLE FISHING BOAT

I STOOD ON DECK FOR SEVERAL HOURS WITH THE GRUMPY FISHERMAN WHO OWNS THE BOAT . . .

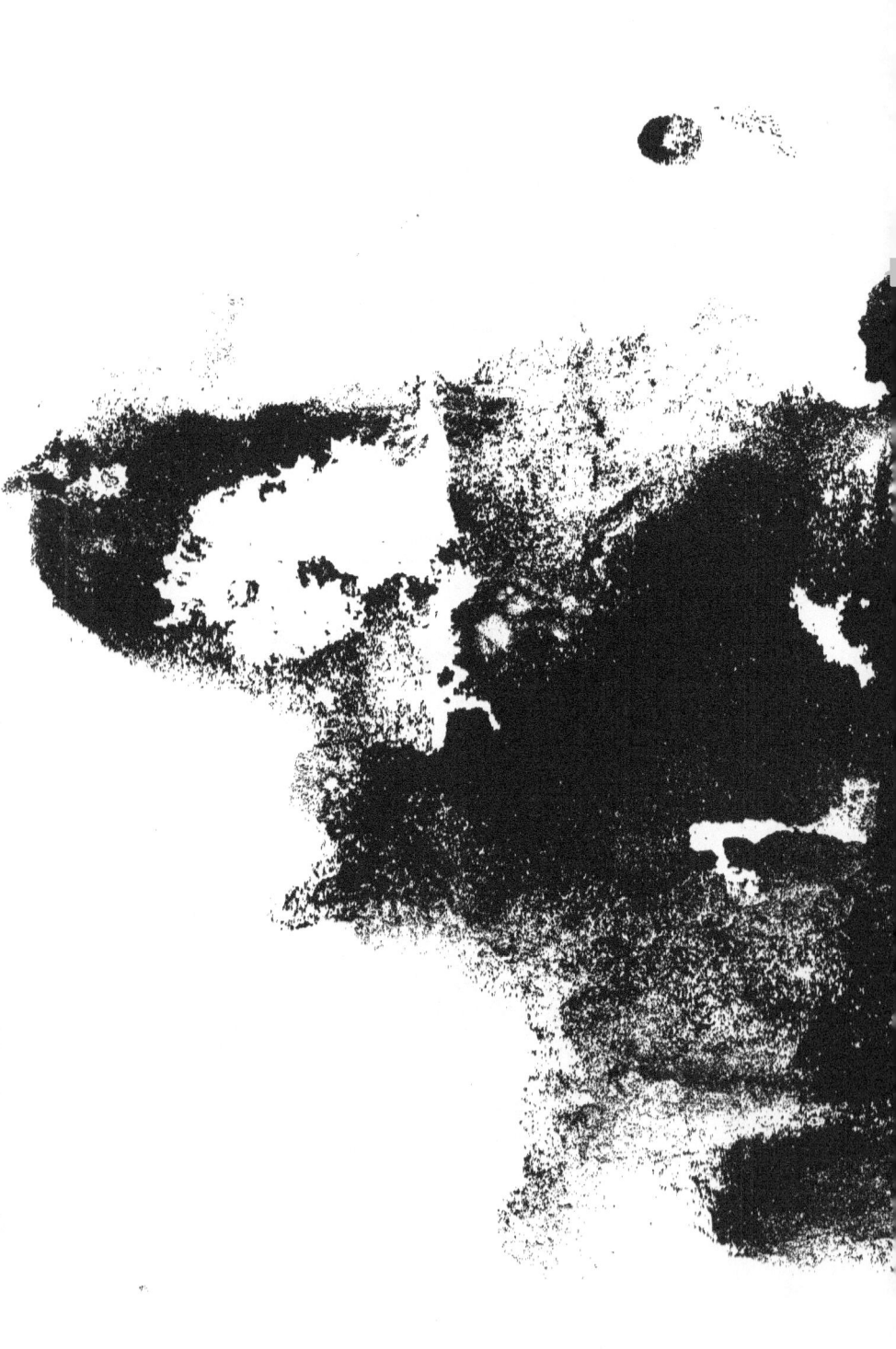

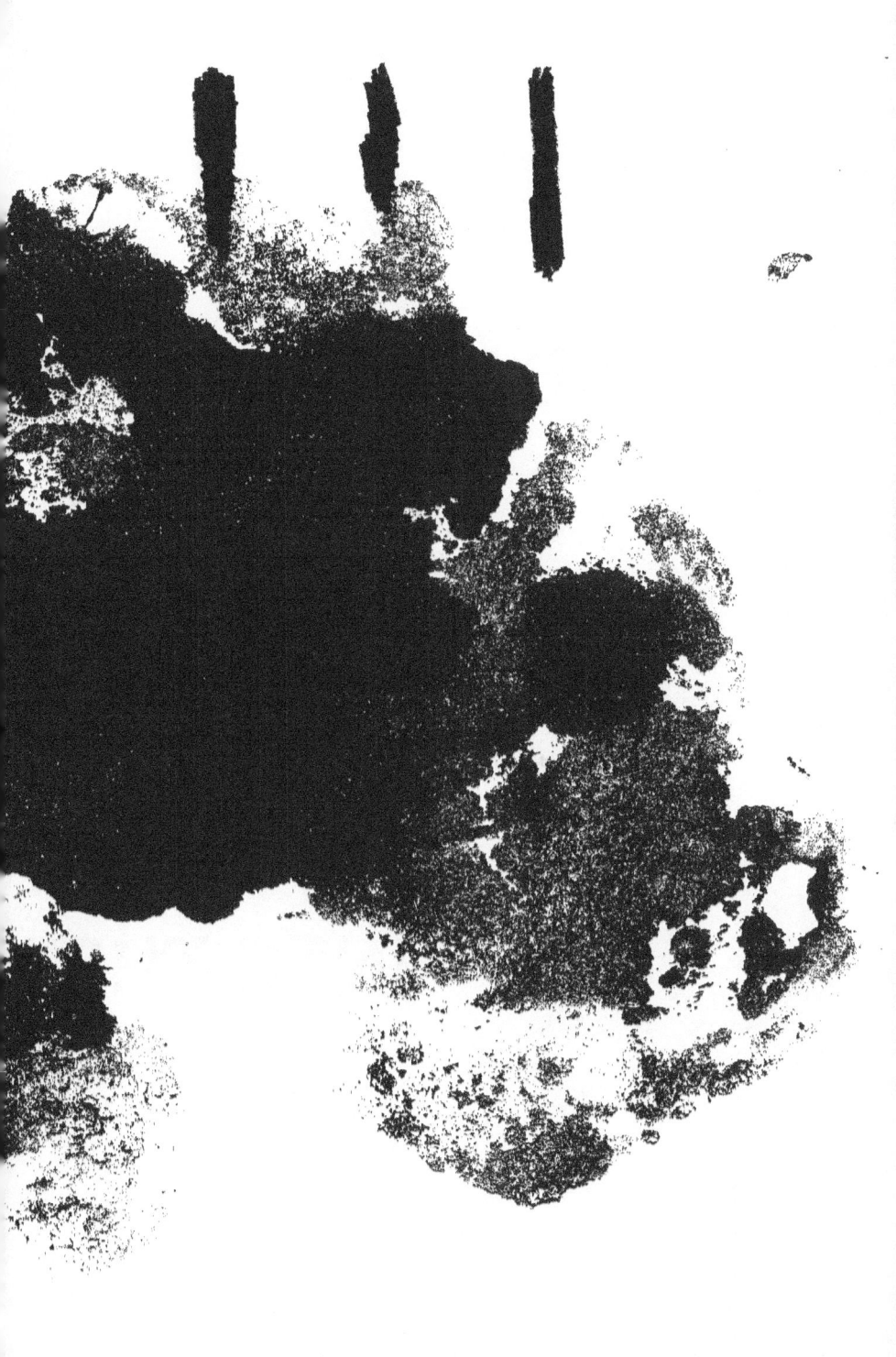

AND WATCHED A
BRIGHTLY
MOVING SLOWLY
EASTERN
AND
INTO THE

DOZEN LINES OF COLOURED DOTS DOWN TO THE TWO HARBOURS DISAPPEARING TRANSPORT SHIPS.

I LOOKED FOR YOU IN EVERY LINE,

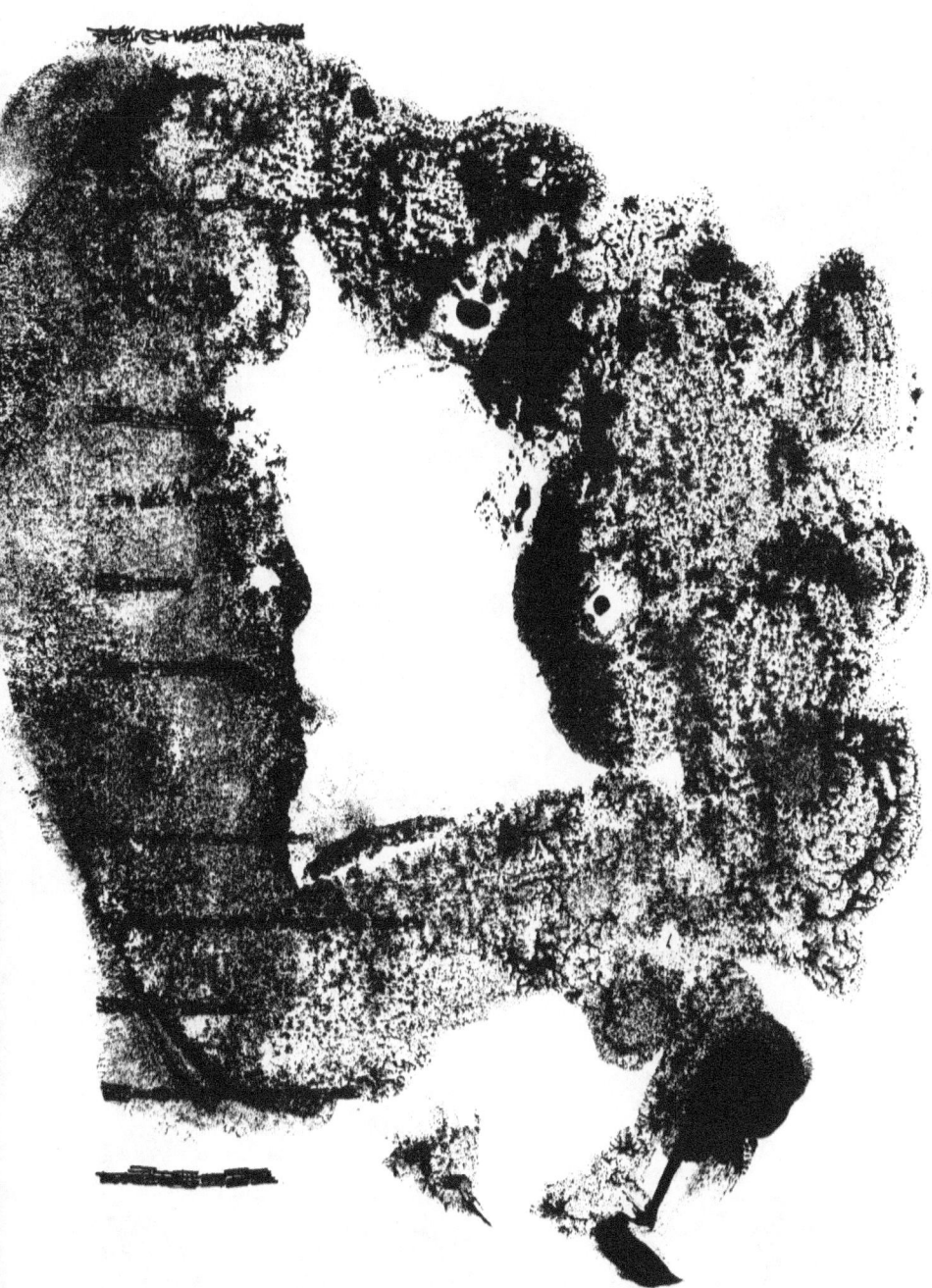

FOR SOME RECOGNIZABLE ITEM OF CLOTHING,

BUT I WAS TOO FAR OUT AND, MADDENINGLY, HAD BROUGHT ONLY THE WEAKEST OF BINOCULARS.

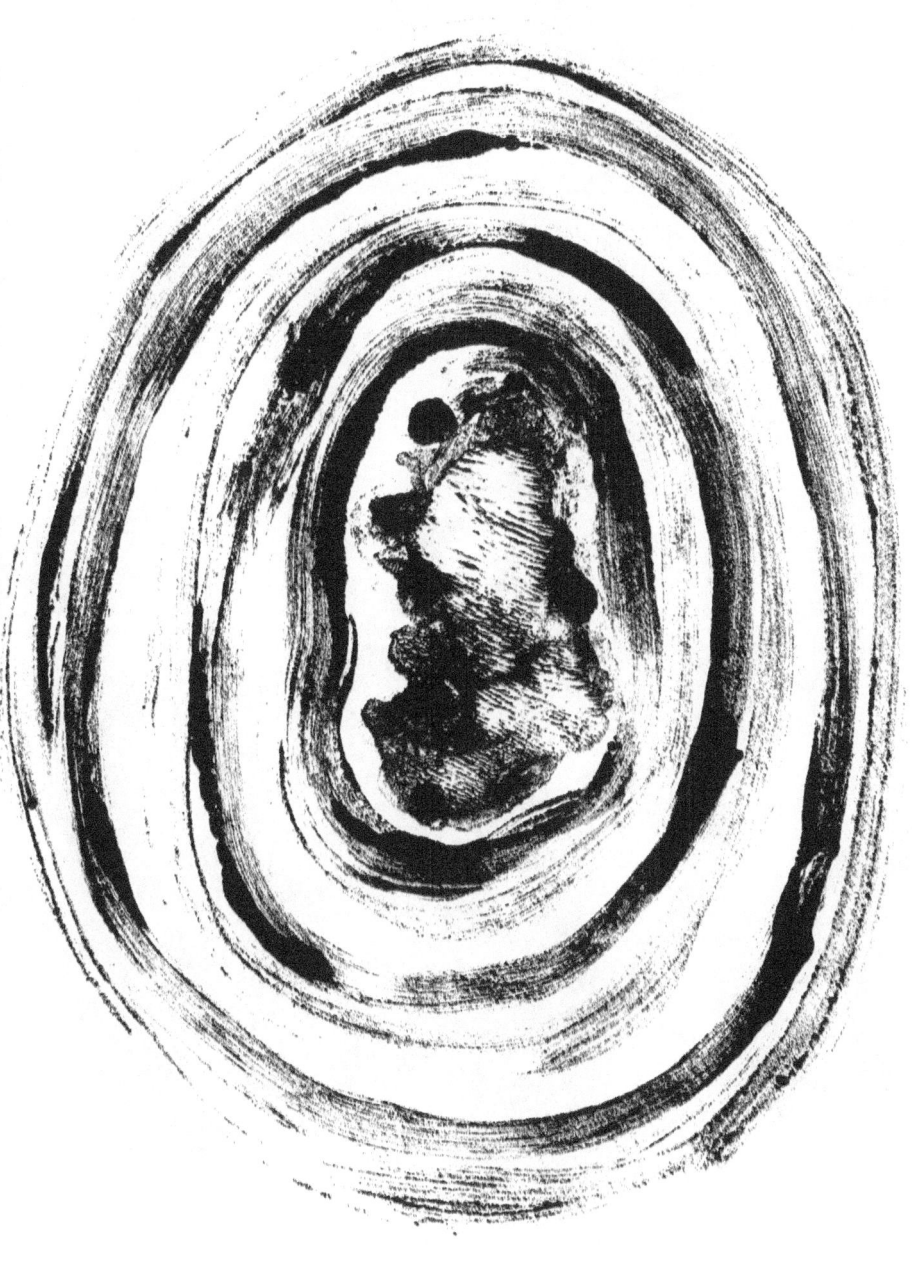

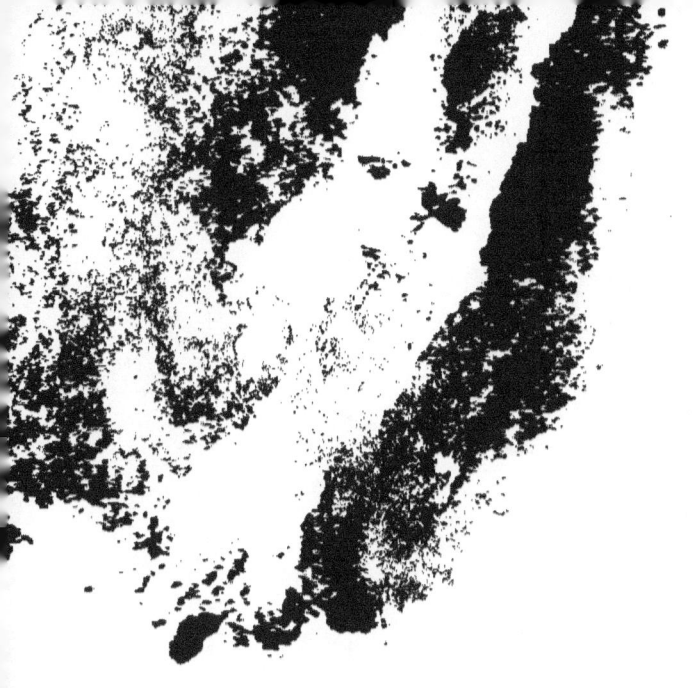

WHEN AT LAST THE SHIPS WERE FULL AND ALL THE COLOUR HAD BEEN DRAINED FROM THE LANDSCAPE,

THE ISLAND DWINDLED BEFORE OUR EYES

UNTIL
IT
WAS
NOTHING
MORE
THAN
A
MEANINGLESS
ROCK.

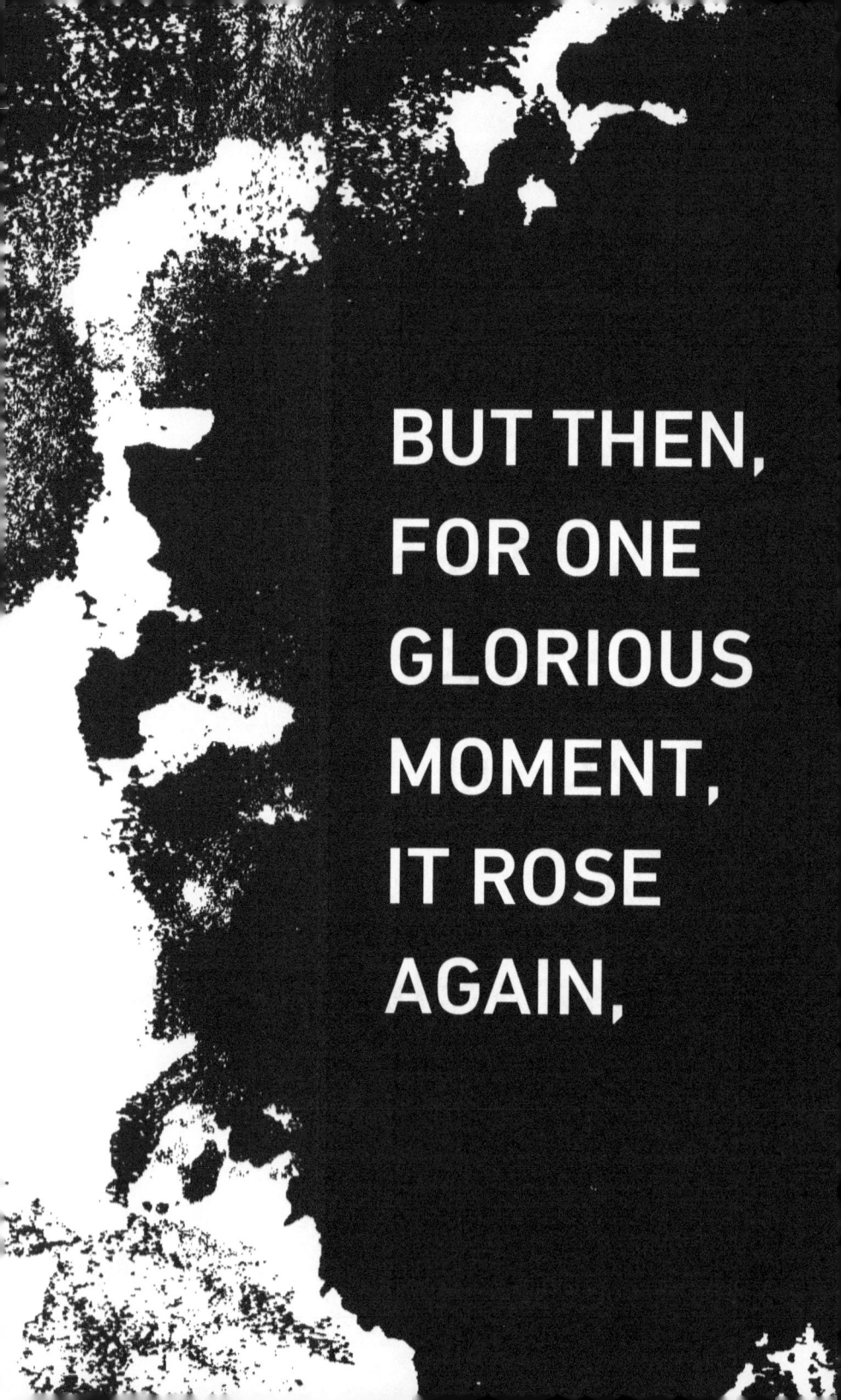

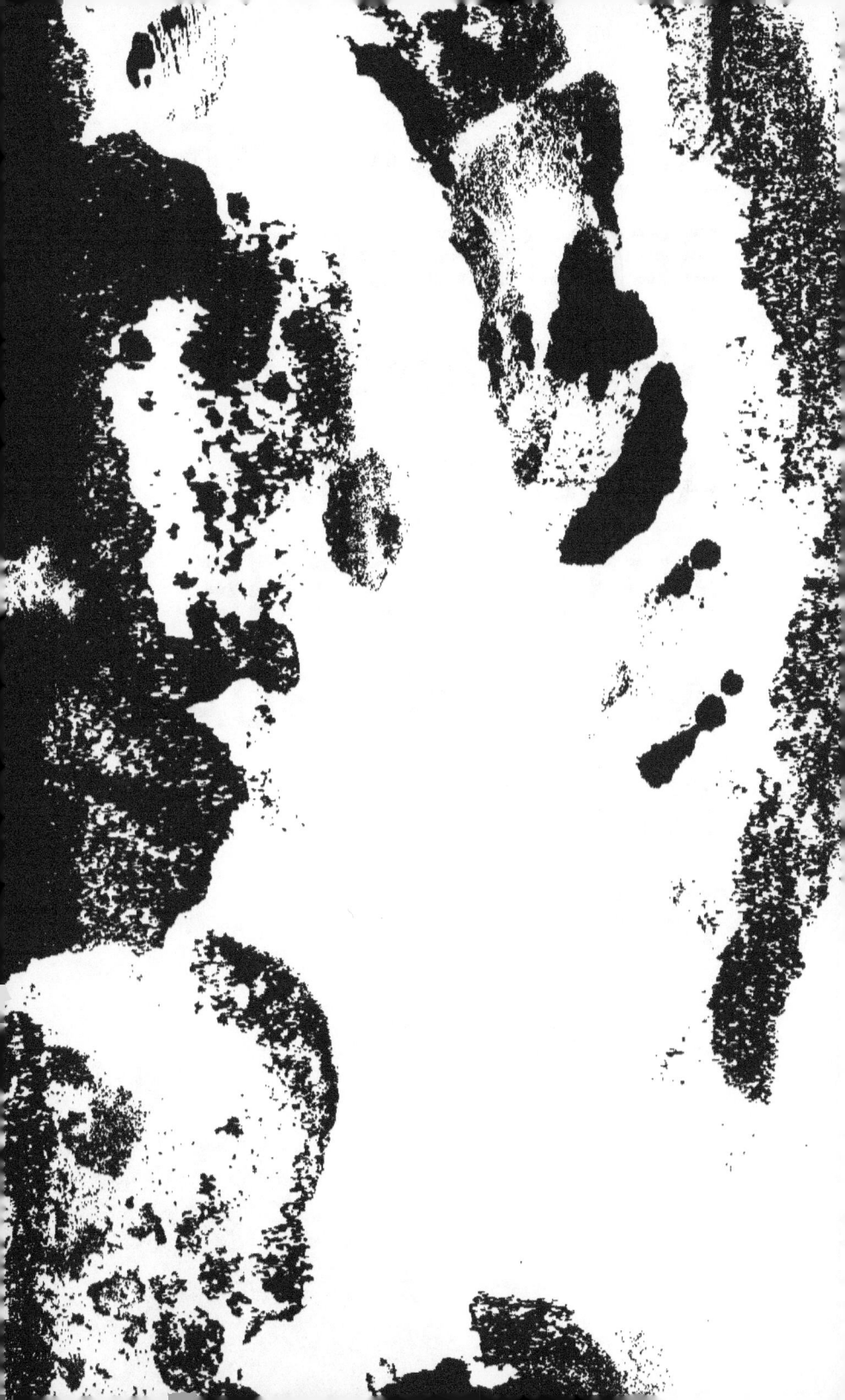

AND FROM THE
BELLIES OF THE
SHIPS AND OUT
ACROSS THE
WATER TO THE
WATCHING BOATS
THERE CAME
THE SOUND
OF SINGING.

AND WE CHEERED UNTIL OUR THROATS WERE SORE.

AND WHEN
WE HEARD YOU
CHEERING IN
RESPONSE,

WE CHEERED
AGAIN.

AND
THEN
THE
SHIPS
MOVED
OFF
IN
ALL
DIRECTIONS

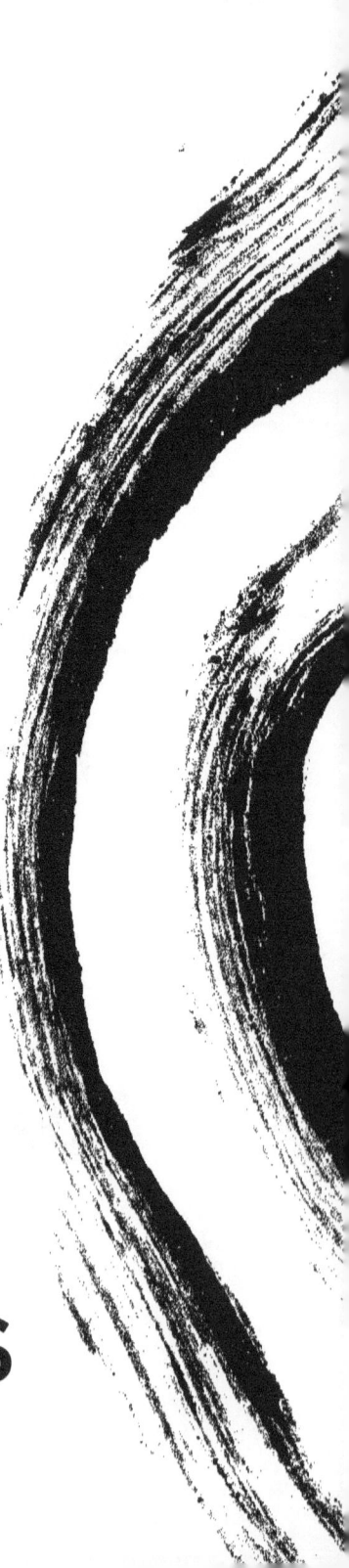

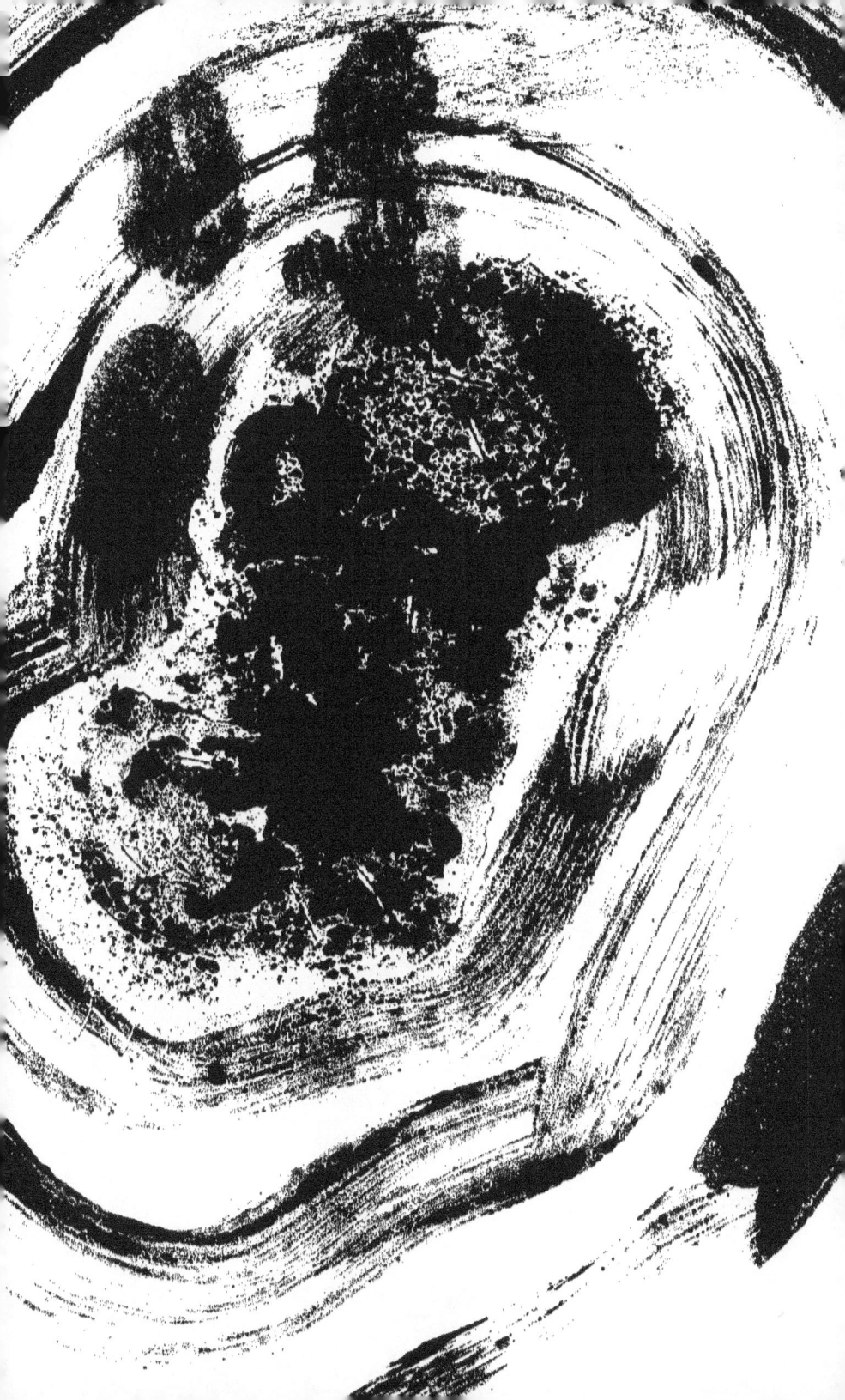

AND THE
ISLAND
DISAPPEARED

FOREVER.

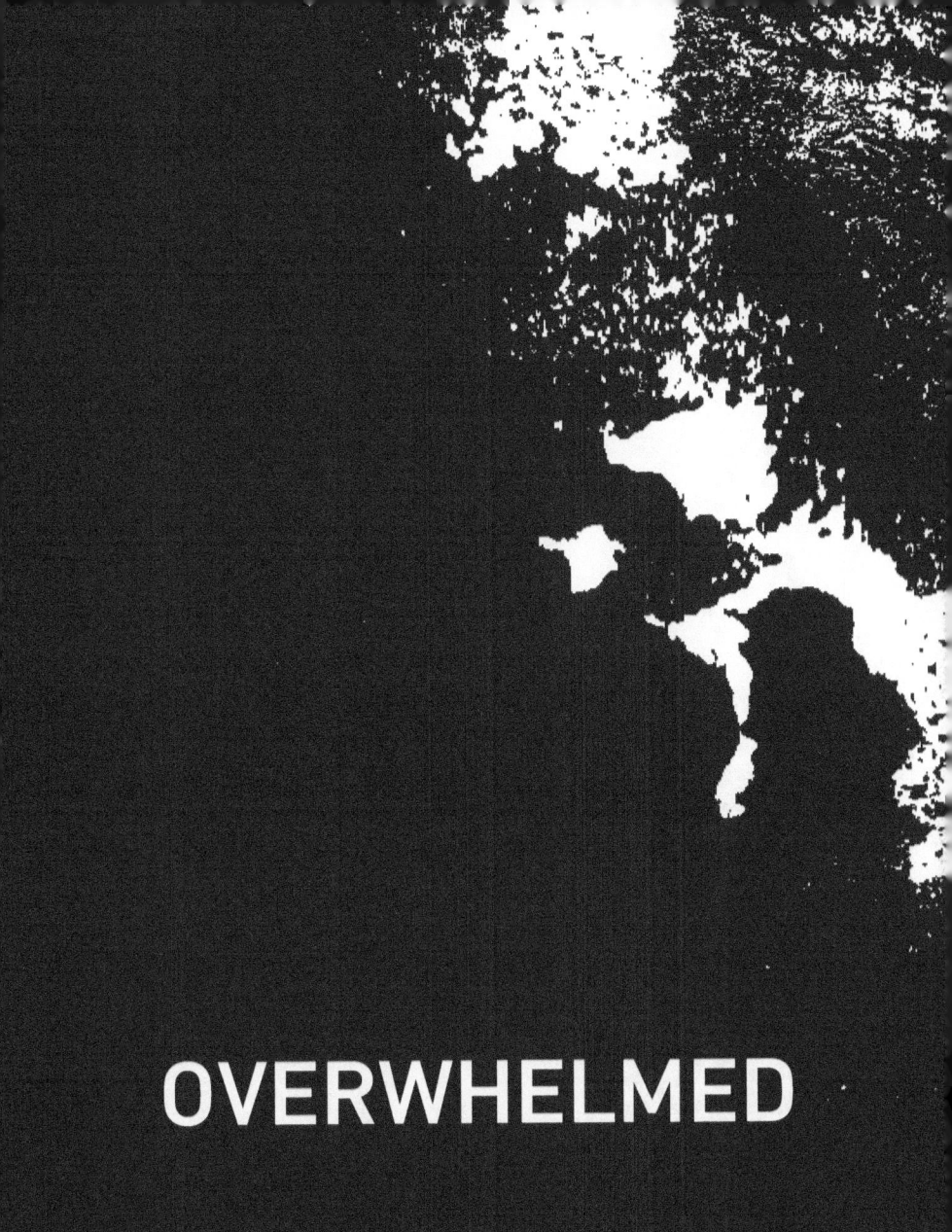

BY
AN
ENORMOUS
SENSE
OF
LOSS,

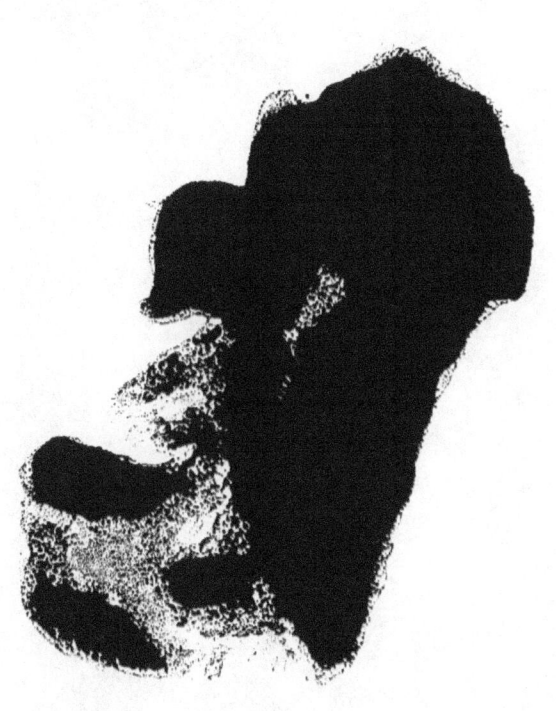

I
WENT
BELOW
AND
WEPT.

www.ingramcontent.com/pod-product-compliance
Lightning Source LLC
Chambersburg PA
CBHW031557210526
45464CB00003B/1319